ABBODIES COLD : SPECTRE

nicky melville

SAD PRESS

978-1-912802-35-7

Bristol 2020

ABBODIES COLD : SPECTRE : 01:10 ^{OO1}

just when ~~you~~ I thought
it was safe
to listen to ABBA again

mamma mia!

here ~~we~~ I go ~~again~~

putting the pop into
apophenia

seeing patterns
that are~~n't~~ there

the spectre
and spectators of fascism
are haunting the world
and the world   is not enough
they want to go
to Mars as well

wtaf!

I must have lit
my seventh cigarette
at half past 2
stopped for 10 weeks
but was crackin up

gave up the drink

for this!

all the powers of the world
have entered into
an unholy alliance
to exercise this spectre

the times change
and we change with them

how much alcohol
~~do~~ did you consume?

too much

there are so many
ways of taking vengeance
on the world   sometimes
literature
is not enough

I was never thinking
of doing
a sequel
to *ABBODIES*
     [like Daniel Craig
     I'd rather slit
     my wrists
     than do an
     other ABBA poem

to be and to not be

but for a price
I'll erase anyone
or thing

I'm nothing special
in fact
I'm a bit of a bore
all I do
is eat and sleep
and write poems
Dr No
body on the line
the one who looks at birds
in order
to predict
the future
I try to capture every minute
the feeling in it

words speak us
pre
diction]
my long poem about
Brexit
bodies
and aliens
viewed through the lens
of 20 ABBA songs

I had to kill

time   till
they named the new Bond film
No Time To Die

and since *ABBODIES*
ABBA have announced two new songs
and have been lured out
to do a virtual tour with avatars
ABBATARS would be better [thanks Steven]

not only that
I've found even more evidence
of aliens in other ABBA songs

in fact
aliens have been known
by our government
since 1905
The Aliens Order Act
amended the law
with regard to
Aliens

and now in the US
(ICE) Immigration
and Customs Enforcement
said 'approximately 680 removable aliens'
had been detained

the truth is out there

but there's a lie in aliens

words are the new weapons
satellites the artillery

in 'I'm a Marionette'
ABBA sing
as if I had come from outer space
        it's obvious that Ulvaeus
        teases us
out of place
        as to his origins

how do you
follow for follow

that!

coming through a cloud
you're looking at me from above
and I'm a revelation

the ABBA song 'The Visitors'
also known as
'The Visitors (Crackin' Up)'
is apparently about
the mistreatment of
political dissidents
in the Soviet Union
it was originally called

'The First'
the first what?
which   semes different
to me

unidentified object on scope
up there

'I'm a Marionette' also mentions puppets
strings and
refugees

and at Christmas
I watched *Spectre* again
the last James Bond film
cause it was on TV
and I remember it being
more misogynistic
than *Skyfall*
        the best modern Bond film imo
        which is nonetheless also problematic
        Bond just rocks up in her shower
        likes her better
        without her Beretta
he smashes the wine glasses
champagne flutes
to be exact
walking toward Monica Bellucci

what would happen

if the sky
did   in
deed fall?

and it crumbles
what then?

I guess we're finding out
now
                              welcome to Scotland! [Albert Finney]
I realised there *was*
a tenuous way in
toward a sequel
via some other
unidentified
folks or other
who run
the world
that is S.P.E.C.T.R.E.
        SPecial Executive for
        Counterintelligence
        Terrorism
        Revenge and Extortion

        number two is in charge
        of the NATO project
and Bond films could also reference Brexit
        love me
        or leave me
        make your choice

        but believe me
for he is forever keeping
the British end up
Queen and cuntry

but ABBA too?

you might not think
there's any more
mileage in ABBA
but I do

I do I do I do I do I do

cuckoo!

so a sequel
of sorts
but
I didn't think it could
also include
aliens
as well

then   in *Spectre*'s opening credits
octopus tentacles
and black ink
do I see the signs
I think
I see

going deeper
below ABBA

Digging [graves]
the dancing [May] queen
no thanks to Theresa
whose dancing isn't as bad
as people say

night is young and
the music's sigh

the aliens in *Arrival*
the film named after the ABBA album
are octopusesque
with 7 legs
the actors call them heptapods
        before ABBA Benny appeared
        in the Hep Stars
        from Hep Stars to heptapods
and their language
is made from black ink
[the aliens'
not the actors']

why octopi?

meeting an octopus is
the closest
we're likely to get

to meeting an intelligent alien

and the SPECTRE logo
is a black octopus
with 7 legs

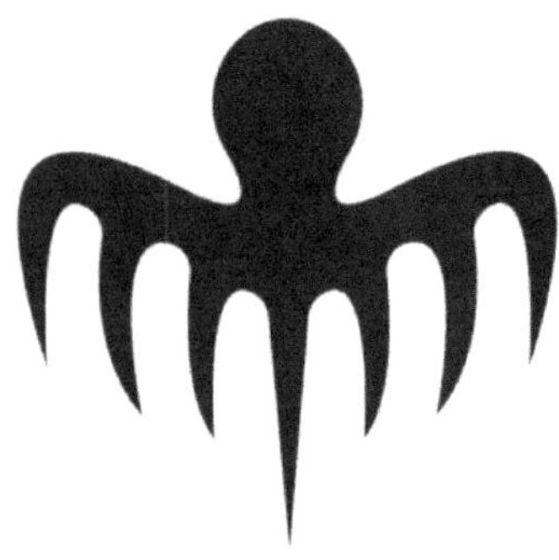

spooky!

it's even more alien in
the '65 version in *Thunderball*
with large grey-like eyes
but with 8 legs

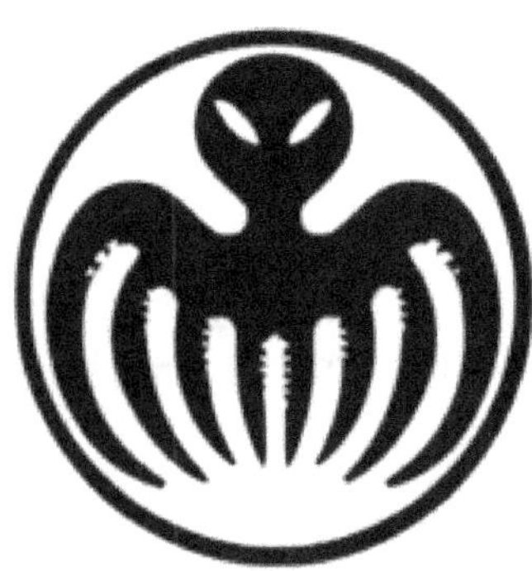

the evolution of cephalopods
yielded
in the octopus
a body of pure possibility

electric lines make the cuttlefish
look like a hovering
space
craft
bright red tails lead
from its eyes
a spaceship crying
tears of blood

and while I was
watching Bond films
taking notes
a virus appeared
in the news
a 'vulnerability'
it's called

Spectre

coincidence?
I think not [002]

and out of nowhere
the other day
my dad asked

if I thought SPECTRE
was behind the poisoning
        from Russia with love
of double agent Sergei Skripal
or is it SMERSH?

he says he didn't know
I was writing a poem
about SPECTRE

maybe he *is* an alien after all

then yesterday
a large hawk-like bird of prey (7)
in the quick crossword

and Blofeld   the head of SPECTRE
asks a question and uses coincidence

did you think it was coincidence
that all the women
in your life
end up dead?

coincidence?

one of my favourite Blofeld scenes
in *For Your Eyes Only*
has Blofeld try
to bribe Bond

they can do a deal
he'll buy him
a delicatessen
in stainless steel

why? lol
what the fuck is Bond
going to do with a delicatessen?

in an interview in *Playboy*
in 1965
promoting *Thunderball*
Sean Connery said
I don't think there'sh anything
particularly wrong about hitting a woman
an open-handed shlap is jushtified
if a woman ish a bitch or hyshterical

#metOO7

in the song for *Thunderball*
Tom Jones
       another pest
sings that Bond is the winner
who takes all

any woman
he wants
he'll get

his days of asking
are all gone

was there ever a man
more misunderstood?

ABBA funded the Swedish
feminist party

£500 please

SPECTRE
is an anagram of
RESPECT

spooky!

S P E C T R E

find out what it
means to me

and in *The Spy Who Loved Me*
a baddies' car drops onto a peasant's house
who comes out and says
Mamma Mia!

coincidence?

and then

the other day
in my inbox
as I was finishing
this beginning
an email from Reed recruitment
        it's time to love Mondays
        Stop faking it
        Try a new position

who's hiring?

MI6

spooky!

Many backgrounds   one
mission

when I typed one
into my old phone
predictive text suggested
obey

but you might not have heard / read
ABBODIES
so you might be
a bit lost

what is to be done?

a spectre is haunting nicky melville
the spectre of *ABBODIES* on the line

I could do a little
previously
like on a TV show

where others
see chaos
I'll see
patterns

for example
the other day
there was a development in
The Digital, Culture, Media and Sport Committee's
Commons investigation into
the Cambridge Analytica
oblique Facebook
scandal
      which involves a Dr Aleksandr Kogan
      who changed his name to Dr Spectre

      coincidence?

Dr Kogan is told
by Committee member Ian C. Lucas (Labour)
'Spectre is also the name
of the evil organisation in James Bond films'

Kogan says that is 'an unfortunate
coincidence'

Cambridge Analytica is not a Bond villain
apparently
Peter Thiel is   probably
and all those other technoid gods

the impending completion
of the global surveillance
initiative will mean
their capability
is second to none

we are submitting
to what
the world has
become

the world is not
enough
in fact
it's too much [003]

ABBODIES previously
on

I was sick and tired
of

a country that works

for everyone
there   is a body on

an ABBA album
        the year I was born

about alien visitors
40 years later

coincidence?

predictive text suggests   invasion

bodies on the line

ABBA's last album
about
aliens   reptiles
disguised as   that!

'S.O.S.' is not about the Brexit

Yes!

I've been broken-hearted
blue
since
knowing me
knowing EU
judges will decide

the likes of me   a body
Oor Wullie

aged 10 years
in one winter

all war
is desire
for millions of bodies
on the line

coincidence?

my dad used to tell me
he was actually
Tom Betteridge
tell me
          what happened
to the wonderful adventures

about my daughter
and son
and you
and
my mother
crying   about
her daughter

I have been waiting
for these V is for visitors

vultures are pretty
        came flying from far away
        now I'm under attack

there is 52% extra

#notnormal signs

I always point out
these common birds of prey
often
in the middle of a   buzzard!

but there will be no buzzards
in this poem
I leave them above us
circling round and round all day
searching for their prey

these last two lines
were written by my sister
in primary 4
in a 4-line poem
about a buzzard

in *The Life of Birds*
David Attenborough
calls raptors   watchers in the sky

and even references my poem

by saying
the adult seeking lizards in the rocks

coincidence?

oh Willie
he's right out   there
he is
behind that rock

Pierce Brosnan
breaks my heart
but not as James Bond
in *Goldeneye* [004]
M calls him a sexist
misogynist dinosaur

reptilian dualism has not
been demonstrated

the common ancestor of birds and humans
     a lizard-like animal
lived 320 million years ago

the common ancestor that
connects
this group to an octopus
     a worm
lived 600 million years ago

her poem had a little drawing too
I remember
my parents stuck it
        the writing's
on the kitchen wall

the buzzard
high in the sky
circling round and round all day
searching for its prey

her teacher   a certain Mr Smithers
said
she didn't write it herself

Nazi or Fazi

I asked her about it
the other day

hey, can you remember
yr buzzard poem? xx

Oh god, goes
something like: the
buzzard circles round
and round all day trying
to catch its prey.

I had: circling round and

round all day /
searching for its prey –
so does it start the
buzzard in the sky or
something? xx

Yeah I think it might be
the buzzard in the sky
way up high, circling
round and round all day trying
to find its prey.

Why? Are you stealing
my work?

ok, thanks. yeah, if you
had read ABBODIES you
would know I write
about buzzards ;) xx

Fuck off you cheeky
bastard. Stop stealing
my work x

stop writing such good
shit then xx

Mr Kiss Kiss Bang Bang

Lol lol x

instead there will be a
cuckoo!
cause I'm a bit
and Blofeld says that to Bond
in *Spectre*

I'm only writing this poem
to get a job
in MI6
what the hell
is he doing   his job

we're all on this earth
to do a job

when you've got a job to do
you've got to do it well
you've got to give
the other fellow hell

where others see chaos
I question

MI6
had an advert on TV
their first ever

there were sharks
and piano music
spookily reminiscent

of the start of 'Skyfall' by Adele

semes to me
not coincidental

seemingly MI6 had a spike
in applications
after the Skripal poisoning

I imagine outraged citizens
around Britain
going

right! that's it
I've had it up to here
with these Russian poisonings
first Litvinenko now this
I'm joining MI6

secretly
they are just
like us

they are intelligence officers
but they don't do
what we think

the voiceover guy kind of laughs
when he says 'don't'

it's not keeping
your cool
in a shark tank

described in the *Guardian* as
sinister music plays as a shark circles

of course
sharks go fin in fin
with James Bond
they're in loads of the films
the baddies put him
in a shark tank
do they expect him to talk?
no
they expect him to be un
able to talk underwater
and maybe get eaten

in *Thunderball*
Largo
  SPECTRE's Number Two
  the NATO guy
has a separate pool
for sharks

I resent that remark

thank you
I'd love to

love to what
dance
at all your Waterloos

oh you're mad
do you know that

yesh ishn't everyone?

[loudly sing] cuckoo!

I thought I could maybe
buy a buzzard t-shirt
for wearing when I read *ABBODIES*
so I searched for one
not knowing whether
they would exist
    now
I know   that adverts
target us through
our online behaviour
but I did not expect
it to extend
to t-shirt design
but I found one mashing
two of my references
buzzards and ghostbusters
into one t-shirt design
Ghost Buzzards

it's true
I'll show it to you

coincidence?

oh and there's a bus tour
in Edinburgh
called Ghost Bus Tours

spooky!

wanted to take the kids
on it
but it would cost £52!

one of my favourite baddies
is Raul Silva in *Skyfall*
played by Javier Bardem

he has metal teeth
due to a cyanide malfunction

chasing spies   so old
fashioned
it's exhausting

when he goes hmmpf
for some reason
he reminds me of Anne Laure
in a good way

and NATO has a designator
for Russia's Burevestnik
nuclear-powered cruise missile
SSC-X-9 SKYFALL

do they always use Bond films to
designate terms for arms
of their frenemies?
as I was writing some new bits
Anne Laure was reading
John Le Carré's *A Perfect Spy*
which I bought for her birthday

the publisher is Sceptre
          I didn't notice till
          I was putting the book in
          my bag
an anagram of Spectre

surely that is
just   a coincidence?

Anne Laure says maybe
she's a spy
to spy on me all these years

semes
sense   to me
why else would she put up with me?

I dislike being spied on
don't we all

Bardem is a nod
to the henchman JAWS
played by seven foot two Richard Kiel
in *The Spy Who Loved Me*
and *Moonraker*
who had metal teeth
and was a nod to JAWS in *JAWS*

my favourite film

coincidence?

and then
the other day
'The Visitors'
an artwork by
Ragnar Kjartansson
was listed as best
of this century
the title 'The Visitors'
is lifted from
ABBA's final album

writing this poem   made me
remember Josephine
whose nickname was Moonraker
        which I did not know

cause she was a witch
I tried to see her
but I was suffering
from a depressive illness
at the time
so nothing happened
can't even remember
if we had a kiss

we're all following
a strange melody
we're all summoned by a tune
we're following
the piper
and we dance beneath the moon

what on earth
are ABBA going on about there?

the history books on the shelves
are always repeating themselves

the UK is going through
the biggest squeeze
on living standards
since the Napoleonic Wars

~~I~~ we've been cheated
by ~~you~~ them
since we ~~I~~ don't know

when

that's all the persons right
there   three
        bodies on the
lines

who are you
and who am I
and who are we

I changed I to we
on the 2nd of September this year
Boris Johnson must come to an end

for the sake of democracy
whatever the hell that is

unlike men
the diamonds linger
[thank fuck]

a Cummings linguist
his organisation
does not tolerate failure

Tory rebels won't feel blue
like they always do

do not let them tell you

we need less surveillance
we need more
much more

world domination
same old dream

his fight goes on and on and on

BJ went to Eton
JB went to Eton
      fucking mess

coincidence?

some people said
I was extreme
for not watching
I'm a Celebrity Get Me Out of Here 2017
because BloJo's father
Stanley was on it

what drives this person
derives from that person

let's blame the father
for a change

as ABBA said
sometimes ~~I~~ they

have toyed
with ideas
that ~~I~~ they got
from good old Freud

one life for yourself
and one for your dreams

there goes that sonofabitching saboteur

England   Empire
you're living in a ruin

we're at an all-time high
for having visible fascists
at large a
round the world
and some of them are very large

Fazis!

they'll change all that's gone
before

make it a September to remember
this is *another* September
and it is memorable

all of us can feel
the autumn chill

earlier   this summer
       hopefully not our last
tourists in Edinburgh became
familiar with that cheeky Scot
Oor Wullie
on his Big Bucket tour
display in the capital
which might help this book
break America
or America break me
Oor Skeleton
App code 2719
his bones have been
put on display
for anatomical study
they glow in the dark

part of Scotland's first
national public art
trail aims to unite the country

James Bond is named
after an ornithologist
       day   wasted
       sky   bird
called James Bond
whose book
Birds of the West Indies
       Pierce Brosnan
       can be seen reading

    in *Die Another Die*
mentions the Turkey Vulture
the only one known there

the Labour leadership
circled over May's
government like vultures
watching a wounded
animal crawl across
an arid plain

a turkey buzzard on the cross

Martin Rowson cartoons
drew Theresa May as a spectre
a ghost tory   love a good
   ghost tory

May plodsded on
in her death spiral
as Farage circle-led
his prey

Keep Calm
and Carrion

try preying
it's easier than
you think

James Bond is just
a stupid policeman
the things he does
for England kills
for queen and cuntry
OO7's loyalty
always to the machine
but then   he *does* stop
SPECTRE and saves
the world from annihilation
and that's good for us
good for the world

for England James
this dear   dear land
dear   for her reputation
through the world
is now leased out

the copyright for the name SPECTRE
was tied up
        much like Bond at times
in legal wranglings
after *Thunderball* in 1965
and only sorted in 2013
freeing it to be
employed
for Bond's last outing

coincidence?

possibly not

in the intro to
the newest edition of *Thunderball*
the book that launched SPECTRE
Barbara Broccoli writes
Fleming fuelled
our paranoid tendencies
by creating SPECTRE

a veritable rainbow
of international bad guys
        under Blofeld
go after the man who holds the whip
somewhere in the world
there is a [pro]rogue
empire being built
in a secret lair
with a mastermind
pulling the strings

whoever controls this data
controls the future

as Roger says
in *Octopussy*
it certainly pays to advertise
what a wise man

we hope that the public

are ready for SPECTRE's resurgence

NATO's number two's ship
is called the Disco Volante

which means
flying saucer

coincidence?

the first ever investigation into flying
saucer
scares
in 1948
was called Project Sign

aha!
ah ha ha

the MI6 job title is
Secret Intelligence Service – Business Support
Officer

sounds like Bond's job
in *Diamonds Are Forever*
he's called in to protect
the diamond mine interests
of Sir Donald Munger

I remember

just before going under
the knife
when I was circumcised
the nurse asked
what I wanted to be
when I grew up
I said an actor
like James Bond

and it's probably not a very good time
for a man to be writing
about his penis

but I'm going to
write
about mine

I have Peyronie's
now
shapeshifting alien body
Peyronie hailed
from Montpellier
      the hospital's named after him
which is where
Anne Laure's from

coincidence?

I had just stopped drinking
when I discovered

this condition
that's what I get
for trying to do
the right thing

outer space echoes
with laughter

a bobby's
on the line

poor willy

having problems keeping it up
Q?

and then
the other day
Mark Zuckerberg says
I owe it all to Spectre

saw the headline
and said
fucking hell

did he mean my half-written poem?
flattered and scared

but I received a message
from Stellan Skarsgård

he's in the *Mamma Mia* films
via *Chernobyl*   who said
naïve idiots
are not a threat
        thank fuck

Spectre's song
is 'Writing's on the Wall'
sung by Sam Smith

nothing against them
but it's not very good
doesn't seem relevant
        what writing?
        what wall?
to its host story

semes this can be understood
after Jacob Rees-Mogg
in his Brexit speech
invoked it

And this *is* the writing
that was written

we are cowering
and terrified of the future

our children and theirs
will judge us in the balance

and find us wanting
as the writing on the wall said
at the feast of Balthazar

they have our future
and our destiny in their hands
for you
I have to risk it all
cause the writing's on the wall

the phrase
means there are clear signs

it looks like
you're beginning
to dissociate

aha!
ah ha ha

another reference
to a reference of a
reference of a ref
errance

we're in it tog
ether

that a situation is going to be
come very difficult
or unpleasant

there'sh a shaying in England
where there'sh shmoke
there'sh fire

fascist!

is the buzzword

England is about
to learn the cost
of betrayal

there are some English customs
that are going to change

yesh darling?

coincident with your cuntry's
one indisputable contribution
to Western Civilization:
afternoon tea

he slaps her

I'm one of the few
who can do
a Sean Connery and
Roger Moore impression
at the same time
though you have to be closhe
to shee my eyebrow action

what is needed is a new story
and one we can believe in
Britain
        a now more or less valueless ally

I want my people
to do the same
says Trump

one of the principal capitalist exploiters
of the West
to show up the incompetence
of the British
the backwardness
of their little Colony

Blofeld's con
trolling it now

we're all just bodies
        on the line
that haven't decayed yet

Blofeld takes over
The Whyte House

you can watch it on TV

this summer in France
we went to the house
of the vultures
and crossed
le bonheur river
happiness river

et aucun oiseaux ne chante

and no birds sing
they are disappearing

what does it do
a   cuckoo!?

the behaviour of
the adult vultures
is interesting

there is no notion of hierarchy   except
the starving one

we are the starving ones
not the vultures

last summer in France
I saw my first honey buzzard

honey honey
how you thrill me
ah-hah
honey buzzard!
nearly kill me

and also the rough-legged buzzard
a beauty
brilliant plumage

perched on a bail of hay

you know
this job of ~~yours~~ mine
it's murder
on relationships

I don't want to
talk
about things
we've gone through

I don't need love
for what good would
love do me

I do want
to fucking talk
about things
we're going through

I do need love

the complication
of ~~that song~~ this poem

breaking up
breaking up
I thought
it was

Kraken up
Kraken up

I remember my dad
took me to see *Clash of the Titans*
starring Harry Hamlin
when I was six
and there was a Kraken in it
unleashed by Poseidon

awaken the Kra-can

I realise these poems
are a lot about me   age 6
     the coming
     of the alien
     is a childhood event
also the year I saw my first Bond film
at the pictures
For Your Eyes Only
back to basics
after the space antics
of *Moonraker*
Scottish singer Sheena Easton
sang the theme tune
and is the only singer of a Bond song
to appear in the titles

my cousin Ryan
who was 7

went to see it before me
and I have a memory
of him saying you could nearly
see Sheena Easton's tits
or maybe he just pointed
down at his chest

and it's true that her
upper torso is bare

anyway   can this be right?
am I remembering correctly?
were we so sexualised by then
or was it just him?
the alien is a child or
the child is an alien

and then my themes conjured
the appearance of
Harry Hill's Alien Fun Capsule
creating magical
moments for families
to stop the alien invasion [005]

take a look at the world
chaos

it's for the kids

what happens next?

it's not personal
it's the future
and you're not

a few years ago
I said when I die
I want to be
left   in a ditch
to be eaten   by birds
and wild animals

the oppressive sense of carrion

names is
for tombstones baby

and now Boris Johnson says
he would rather die in a ditch
      this bless-ed plot
than seek an extension

faces
facts

coin
cidence?

money money money
this happy little breed of men

this spectred isle
    your pitiful little
    island
    hasn't even been
    threatened
this field of Mars
this earth
this realm
this England

I would rather
he die in a ditch as well

Alas
since Waterloo
one can never
underestimate the English

and then
this today
in my junk mail
HomeHawk HD Cam from@gdfgdfdgf.com

the vultures
will eat ~~y~~our bodies
bones dropped
by [squeamish] ossifrage
onto a smashing talus

hard times

are quickly
forgotten
in times of plenty
[for some]

it's a good time
to be a vulture

after I started thinking about
heptapods and octopi
I minded *Stranger Things*
also has a tentacular creature
the mind flayer [not flare]
and *Ghostbusters*
[easy 80s ref
but ties in nicely
with my poem's themes
perhaps *too* nicely]
and JAWS 006

tentacular evil
takes many forms
and 80s capitalism
may just be one of them

it didn't come
from Russia
it came
from here

where would Russian research be
without Silicon Valley?

silicon is common sand

apophenia
is explained in season three

coincidence?

and bald eagle
as codename
allegory

critics may accuse me
of self-indulgence
and suggest
I am
bald eagle
Blofeld
or Dr Evil
just cause I'm bald

[haters back off]

a delirious Christopher Walken
the villain in *A View to a Kill*
    Natalie Wood   what happened there?
attempts to
destroy silicon valley

why is this a bad thing?

I also watched
Life is Strange
a walk around
game
that my son loves

because I wanna know
what's the name
of the game
theory
[asymmetrical poetry]

release the Kraken
is a refrain in it
for some reason

Chloe says release the Kra-can
when she gets some pop
from the juice machine

we don't have
all the time
in the world is
not enough

that's Garbage

there's a whole world

out there

it's for the kids

in these old familiar rooms
children would play

sorry kids
I had to go

already my children's ghost

Winter Light
tonight's Swedish obsession

Mr Persson
is worried about red China
and atomic bombs

nothing changes
everyone feels this
dread

why must I suffer so
hellishly
for my insignificance

it's like a mirror
of my mind

prepare for the invasion

there's a clip of Bjorn
in the BBC ABBA doc
doing an ad
for a programme called
Countdown
        but not the C4 show
        that launched
        alien pundit
        Carol Vorderman
isn't *Countdown* a great
great show
for these great times

Brexit is scheduled for 31st October
Halloween

spooky!

i con
cidence

scary
very scary

watching the
last debate
in parliament
the house of horrors

on the eve of its pro
roguing

England is a sick nation
by any standards
by hastening the sickness
to the brink of death
might Britain not be
forced
out of her lethargy
into the kind
of community
effort we witnessed
during the war?

stop it
you're
like boys
with toys

the Prime Minister
has made his water
loo   [Phil Wilson   Labour]

has met his destiny
in quite a similar way

my whole career
is on the line
here

David is on the bridge
    still   he lives
    somehow
just down from the nightly
soup kitchens   prelude
to revolution
bread of apocalypse
the aristocracy waving
alms-bags   food banks
now
in front for a banner

maybe I should give
a fiver for using him
in my poems 007

finally
the US navy
admitted UFO films
which were 'leaked'
are real
    coincidence?
but are now known
as Unidentified Aerial Phenomenon

and finally
finally
in today's crossword
a laugh (5)
Te-Hee

in a country where men all [sic]
sleep
in their grave-clothes
and like phantoms
communicate by signs

language says UFOs are ways
for folk to release anguish
in the face
of modern scientific changes
fear of war and atomic catastrophe and

the my inability
to adapt to
the present rhythm of life

one of the villains in
Live and Let Die
along with   Amity
     for friendship (5)
the name of the island
in *JAWS*

coincidence?

no aliens   but
I've been expecting you

this September   is
preparedness
month
and as I finished this
pairs of Chinooks
     Soldiers write the songs
     that soldiers sing
     the songs that you
     and I don't sing
flew over my flat
daily
what's up with that?

buzzards!

END [TIMES] NOTES

OO1

Time parliament reconvened for its proroguing on September 10th 2019. This morning it was judged unlawful by the supreme court.

OO2

Nothing is connected to everything is connected to something. My magical thinking led me to chaos magic which referenced Arthur Koestler's *The Roots of Coincidence*. There is no coincidence, only the illusion of coincidence. Perfect. I'd never heard of this book, but knew Koestler was into the paranormal, there's a parapsychology unit at the University of Edinburgh named after him. I've done some volunteering for it. Including a sleep experiment investigating precognition in dreams. It was weird as. Kind of worked. There was a creepy researcher who suggested he come to my flat and do experiments while I slept, if I was interested in more. Anyway, at 11.25 on the morning of the 13th of June I decided to look this book up on Edinburgh City Libraries' website. It said the online catalogue was unavailable from 11 a.m. *that day* to 5 a.m. the next. Coincidence? When it came back online the book was listed, so I noted the shelf mark and went to Central Library to look for it. Wasn't there, must be stored off-site. NBD. I also looked for a Kei Miller book which I needed in preparation for the Scottish Universities' International Summer School (SUISS), where I teach. That wasn't there either. When I got home I reserved both books. Concurrently, I was reading *V for Vendetta* also in preparation for SUISS, the first graphic novel I'd ever read (though I'd seen the film, which wasn't great). In it, one of the characters is reading—you couldn't make this up—*The Roots of Coincidence*. Wonderful books these, Koestler and Boronowski. WTAF! Meantime, I checked to see if the books had arrived at the library, shouldn't take too long. I looked up my reservations and Kei Miller's book was in transit, but the Koestler book was nowhere to be seen. No mention of it. So I went back to the library and explained and was told that that must mean it couldn't be found. Single coincidences are merely tips of the iceberg—tip of the tentacle—which happen to catch our eye because we tend to ignore the ubiquitous manifestations of seriality. The visible traces of untraceable a-causal principles in the universe. I just can't tell what's made up and what's real anymore. Coincidence my arse.

This poem has grown arms and legs, particularly legs. Here are the cuts that didn't make the final book: last summer at SUISS my leaving gift was George Oppen's *Selected Poems*, New Directions edition. Someone, I can't remember who, Calum, Ariel or Sarah, opened it at random, and there in the poem 'FROM VIRGIL' was a buzzard. Coincidence? I, says the buzzard / I—. When I read it I also found a spectre. The Thirties. And / A spectre. One of my students this year, Kirsten, wrote in a poem 'chance events are born of fate / and fate is born of Mars.' Not knowing that I was going to mention Mars and chance [coincidence] in this poem. Only called 'chance' or 'coincidence' because its causality has not yet been discovered. What links poetry and dinosaurs? A pterodactyl! M's late husband was a great lover of poetry: that which he was he was. Daniella Bianchi is one of my favourite Bond girls. Victor Tourjansky as Man with Bottle (Uncredited) in *The Spy Who Loved Me*. No room for Alan Partridge—ah-hah!—who links both Bond and ABBA. He's a Roger fan as well. Not being English / I sometimes find your sense / of humour rather difficult / to follow. The concept of the reptilian mind. Answer: buzzard! Of course. Possible buzzard twice in *Wild Strawberries*. Also in *The Big Short*, *Caddyshack* and *XX*. Other films and programmes I mention in other poems. Then I realised it's just a sound effect. These buzzard sounds are not real. The birds don't exist [*Resolution*]. But why? Why is the mewl of a buzzard used so often in so many places? Sound effects folk have been rumbled, I get the message. This is the increasingly mature nature of my material. Watching the ABBA documentary with neon blue subtitles in case I miss things. *Tomorrow Never Dies* was originally meant to be *Tomorrow Never Lies*. Someone misread the fax. Remember them? Faxes. Carver ~~Murdoch~~ has an edifice complex. The Bond films are generally pretty shit. They are like naïve dreams. Roger is still king. As Alice Tarbuck rightly said: fandom's greatest achievement / has been / James Bond / as somehow redeemable / as humanised / as interesting / and complex / that and all / the great / considered / body-diverse / consensual / fascinating / hot-as-hell sex. Marx approved of the methods of the German Workers' Educational League: study not conspiracy. They go hand in hand. Fear is not good for the serenity of research. And there's a meme of the walking contortionist from the hotel entertainment complex at Martinique in *Live and Let Die*. Tristan saw it earlier the day we watched it. An example of recency illusion. Te-Hee! In Fleming's *You Only Live Twice*—totally different from the film, at some point he is overhung, mouth like a vulture's crutch—a fishing cormorant is named after the film star David Niven, who would go on to play Bond in the first *Casino Royale* film three years later (a parody made after the first four Bond films). Coincidence? And Elon Musk's SpaceX has a reusable heavy-lift launch vehicle called Falcon

Heavy. Get him off that machine isn't a DeLorean. What does that mean? Back to the Future. Timothy Dalton, just in case he feels left out. His films are ok, better than Brosnan's. But I didn't have enough time or money to watch any. This never happened to the other fellow. George Lazenby. In case he feels left out too. I can only hope your presence here is a coincidence Mr Bond. Kogan is obviously lying. The doctor he supposedly named himself after is Dr Spector, different spelling. Thought I'd better put in Putin. They're everywhere. Those Russians ['Rasputin']. They have someone in every room. Am I right? Asks Mr White. Lotte Lenya was a diseuse, a 'teller'—they have them in parliament too—she punched an oiled-up Robert Shaw [Red Grant] on SPECTRE island in *From Russia With Love* with a knuckle duster. A fine specimen. A new super race of perfect physical specimens. I was wrong about ABBA's relationships in *ABBODIES*. Agnetha and Bjorn got divorced in 1979 just as Anna-Frid and Benny got married and they divorced in 81. My mum in case she feels left out. Aislinn also. I was reading Donna Haraway's 'Tentacular Thinking: Anthropocene, Capitalocene, Chthulucene' for the tentacles. Halfway through I had a pause and went for a pee and started thinking of another Donna, the one that's in *It's A Wonderful Life*, and it took me a while to think of her surname, Reed, but I got there in the end. Then I went back to the essay and the next footnote referenced a filmmaker called Donna Reed (and also Starhawk, a neopagan author and activist). This is an example of what Jung calls synchronicity. The face is familiar, as is the manner. When an unexpected mental content which is directly or indirectly connected with some objective external event coincides with the ordinary psychic event. I am the (synchroni)city. Fowler once said I was the city (Edinburgh), but he doesn't dare to come here anymore now, cause he put Calum's body on the line. Junk mail for size? with a subject that says NEWarrivals? See what's just landed. You have arrived at a propitious moment. Victor Tourjansky as Man with Bottle (Uncredited) in *Moonraker*. At the end of which it says it was filmed on location in ITALY, BRA-SILIA, GUATEMALA, USA and OUTER SPACE! There's also a reference to *Close Encounters of the Third Kind*. One fascinating example of synchronicity is that both physicists and para-psychologists used the term 'psi' to indicate what is still unknown. Jacob Rees-Mogg as Vampire squid with Top Hat. The word eidolon. Am I the only one who thinks 'Money Money Money' sounds like the theme tune for *Inspector Gadget* which has a Blofeld parody in Dr Claw and is the head of M.A.D. Which no one knows the meaning of. The delicious octopus salad we now make. As I write, a handful of defence lawyers from the military tribunals under way in Guantanamo Bay gathered by James Bond's silver Aston Martin in the lobby of Washington's new International Spy Museum. You can forget the spooks Quarrel. 'Letter Against Spectres' and Sean Bonney's *Ghosts*. Then I find out that cockney geezer Danny Dyer—darling of the media since he criticised David Cameron for Brexit sitting with his trotters up—believes in aliens and says he feels like a ghostbuster. *And* he's related to King Edward III. Honestly, is someone taking the piss? That, the buzzard t-shirts, the new ABBA songs, *Harry Hill's Alien Fun Capsule*, the cephalopods everywhere, and all the rest, really makes me wonder. If aliens *do* come calling, the last thing we've to do is have a referendum about it, according to a recent poll. As an aquarian I am basically an alien in retro gear. My publisher doesn't remember writing a *Ghostbusters* reboot gender flip review. I was thinking about 80s themed nostalgia fests such as *Stranger Things* and *Dark*, the far superior German programme. Is it so the writers can make nuclear and Russian references, not so subtly cloaking analogies with now? Wait. *ABBODIES* and this poem are also nostalgia fests. I guess I am a tool too. Berliners referred to a cigar-shaped UFO as a 'holy ghost.' They don't know shit about outer space. Ufologists. Urologists. My urologist's a mister not a doctor, somehow, encouraging privatisation by stealth, directing me to iMEDicare.com. Good lord bacon, I'm ready to nosh again. Don't make me backwash this bacon. ABBA is also a cleaning company. Some of *The Spy Who Loved Me* was filmed at Faslane. Royal Navy and Shell are thanked in the credits—culture and military industry collusion writ large. Great men have always man/ipulated the media to save the world. The Bond books are known as racist, homophobic, sexist, misogynistic, but they're also anti-Semitic. The Family is a group with tentacles around the world. When they talk of the death of their leader Doug Coe, they say 'three months before he left the earth.' Where did Doug go? There is some consolation in that. May they squirt inky night into the visualizing apparatuses of the technoid sky gods. When they had to dig in, when they had to defend, when they had to put their bodies on the line and do it right. Alan Shearer talking about the England football team. After ABBA won the Eurovision Stockholm hosted the next one and there was an alternative, doing the immoral song contest. Maud Adams is actually Swedish! As Swedish as meatballs. So is the other Bond girl in *Octopussy* Kristina Wayborn. Four things that Sweden is famous for abroad: glass, free sex, drunkenness and suicide. Got ill blood relatives. Too depressed to listen to ABBA at the moment. You know you're hurting when you don't give a shit about music. Why do we have to go on living? SUISS idle thoughts: deep/rest. Putting you out of my misery. Anthony Burgess worked on the script for *Thunderball* and he has a book called *ABBA ABBA* but doesn't even mention the Swedish pop sensation once! Sven Olaf Waldorf dressed as Napoleon. I was going to subtitle this *Mamma Mia 2*, to try and cash in on the sequel to *Mamma Mia*. It can be *Mamma Mia 3*. Is it coincidence that the codename for the UK Treasury's cross-government civil contingency planning for the possibility of a no-deal Brexit is called Ope**ration** Yellowhammer, named after the farmland bird, the bunting, the yellowhammer, whose song is generally transliterated as 'a-little-bit-of bread-and-no-cheese'? I think not. It's also known as 'deil-deil-deil-tak ye' in Scots. Fuck this! Get the bunting out! The fact that I cut into the future with my harvested wordsmash—Are vultures future?—*The Imperative Commands* using Calum and Sebastian Charles's Dada machine. This predates the buzzards and vultures of *ABBODIES*. A magical response to the time and hawks to come. Silicon-based intelligence is a thing. Trump told May he doubted Russia was behind Skripal attack. Vulture funds undermine the development of the most vulnerable. This is from *Winners Take All* by Anand Giridharadas to which my magical thinking led me. Vulture funds routinely buy bad debt at a steep discount and then sue African governments to repay them in full with taxpayer money. In the Highlands a buzzard is known locally as the tourists' eagle. Waterloo is also mentioned in *JAWS* in a classic speech delivered by Quint [Robert Shaw], the same scene where 'I've got that beat' appears [see end times note OO6]. The script was rewritten by Robert Shaw who led the shark hunt. He was followed around on set to make sure he didn't get drunk. I had forgotten Telly Savalas was a Blofeld, we'll cut him off at the precipice. And then today [this is actually today, unlike some of the other todays, which have slipped due to all the time that's passed—Ivor Cutler again (last seven words only)] spam in my email inbox, an offer of a loan from Falcon Credit Management CEO Damian Falcone only 3% interest on loans from $10,000 to $50,000,000. Pretty fair. Worth giving some thought. Fat chance I'll get a bank loan. Local names include Crow, John Crow and Carrion Crow. John Maus. Those eyes won't leave [read] my mind. I just discovered his apocalyptic music this September. It really helped me focus at the end. But it's too late to reference him. This poem is screen memories. I read that his PhD is called 'Communication and Control' *after* I'd added those words from Norbert Weiner. Coincidence? Fuck Hughes and his hawk in the rain and Yeats and his falcon in its widening gyre. I have been seeing a gyre in real life. A spiral shape in various cultural products: *Life is Strange*, *Pet Sematary* and *The Great Hack*, also others I forget. It was noticed at large in *Game of Thrones*. What does it mean? Your pets are goanna die. Furred spectres. First there was the dream. Now there is reality. All the production setbacks for the new Bond film, far too many to mention here. Why doesn't Blofeld just kill James Bond? So annoying. Roger Moore promoting *A View to a Kill* on the Wogan show, appeared alongside Benny and Bjorn promoting *Chess*. The Spectre video was made by a team including the artists Bill Posters and Daniel Howe and the advertising company [un]Canny. Maybe you two could debrief each other in Guantanamo [film made in 1995 six years before 9/11]. It's not a good time for paranoids, never is, densely packed with gas and rock. Victor Tourjansky as Man with

Wine Glass (Uncredited) in *For Your Eyes Only*. Universal exports is Bond's cover persona. Where the fuck will the exports be going now? Instead of play on the Bond DVDs it's initiate mission. Language decryption. I was Victor Tourjansky. I'm Alan Partridge. Alien ABBAductees report missing time and paralysis. I've had plenty of both but the main cause was wine. *The Man with the Golden Gun* as remake of *The Wicker Man*: Christopher Lee with a scantily clad Britt Ekland luring a copper [Bond] by seaplane to an island. Word capitalises Beretta! In other words, it's in its lexicon. Kraken Mare on Titan. *Kill 'em All* poster on the wall in *Dark*. Ted Danson in *The Good Place* says we have Nazis again, somehow. A direct reference to contemporary America, got nothing to do with the series. John's falafel prophecy @falafelprophecy. Sometimes I've hawked books to get some cash. 'Vultures in every venture' is stated in the trailer for [t][he] [c][urrent] [w]ar. There's a hovercraft in *Diamonds Are Forever*! I had forgotten such a thing existed. Stromberg wishes to conduct his life on his own terms and in surroundings with which he can identify. That is a privilege of wealth. Sounds familiar. England that was wont to conquer others has made a shameful conquest of itself. The Google doodle for World Teachers' Day is a bald bespectacled octopus with seven legs, in other words: a heptapod. Coincidence? The Arrival is over. And it was actually on the same day as James Bond Day [whatever that is and wherever it came from]. Super coincidence. And then three days later it was World Octopus Day! Bond says put it down to 'Funny Coincidence Department.' What's landed this week Nicholas? September is preparedness month now according to Police Scotland. Since when? And for what? Check your Grab Bag. Police Scotland: Keeping people safe, since 1ˢᵗ April 2013. Note the foolish date. Keeping what people safe from what? Nearly 8 in 10 Americans believe in angels. Have that ready for army day. UK retail sales hit by 'spectre' of no-deal Brexit. What is going to happen is   suspense. In   formation is all, is it not? Caroline Munro [and Dusty Bin] from *3-2-1*. What a handsome craft. Where is the craft?

OO4

It's total nonsense *Goldeneye*, but at least it was worth watching for this line (and a few others). And there's a kind of buzzardy mewl in a night scene [I've written about the implausibility of buzzards at night elsewhere, not least the lack of thermals]. Bond gets in front of Sean Bean's fast-moving train in a tank when it looks like miles away from the city centre where they just were. How did he even find it? Why can't things be a bit more realistic? Ian Fleming had an estate in Jamaica that he named Goldeneye after Operation Goldeneye, a Second World War era contingency plan he developed in case of a Nazi invasion of Gibraltar through Spain. The malware Petya (also known as 'Goldeneye') is a reference to the film. It is also the name of a duck.

005

The premise is Harry keeps the alien invasion at bay by putting funny stuff in his fun capsule. Must keep the aliens happy by giving them a laugh. What happens next? Scottish stuff gets in the fun capsule of course. And then at one point there's a skit where he gets the guests to act as disabled folk as lizards and able-bodied people are the snakes trying to keep them down, then they crowd round Harry as aliens chase him. You couldn't make this shit up. He's bonkers. But good though. He asks the questions but he answers to no one.

006

I've always thought Hopper in *Stranger Things* was Chief Brody (from *JAWS*)-esque—jeep and jacket. In fact, his name is a dicotyledon of Hooper, the ichthyologist character in *JAWS* played by a coked-up Richard Dreyfuss. No knowledge is ever wasted. Then there's a proper bit of plagiarism/allusion when someone says 'I've got that beat.' Exactly what Hooper says to Quint when comparing scars. It can't just be coincidence. [This isn't me, it's another line from *Stranger Things*.] *JAWS* is my favourite film, as I said, and now it's being quoted. Then, 'he's certifiable,' another direct lift, Roy Scheider [Chief Brody] to and about Quint. And there's gallons of *JAWS* referencing in *Life is Strange*, then actual 'sharks.' The shadow of a great white has been significant to me. It was there on a number plate driving back from the City Hospital the morning I first lost it, thinking the porters were out to get me. Wee Bob saying something about a sausage which I took to mean castration. Life is strange. And then, a couple of days after I had discovered all these hidden and not so hidden *JAWS* allusions, Katy Hastie wrote Jaws, instead of Jaqs, in an email to me. Spooky!

007

I gave him a two pound coin just after I'd finished this poem. It was all I had at the time. He seemed pleased and surprised. His voice. He's in some state.

nicky melville will return in ABBODIES MORE COLD

Written on location in Scotland.
The producers would like to thank Creative Scotland, OMEGA® Watches, Aston Martin and the City of Edinburgh.
Acknowledgements: a small section of this poem was published in *The Scores* under the name Nick Nack Melville.

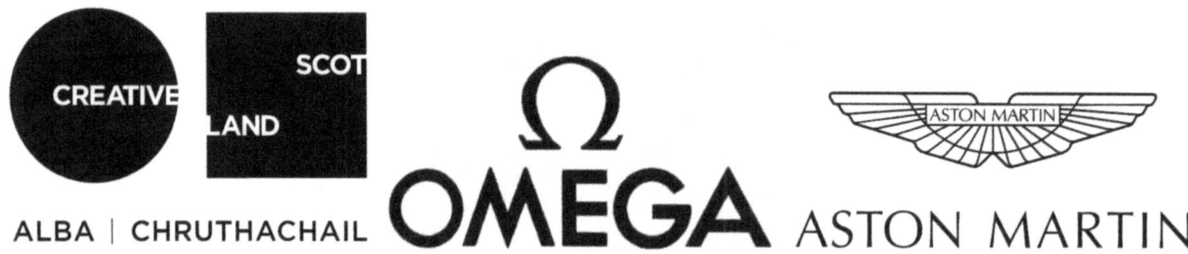